Three Perch Swimming

By Bedell Phillips

Three Perch Swimming
©2022 by Bedell Phillips

ISBN: 978-1-958669-03-7

Published by Piscataqua Press
An imprint of RiverRun Bookstore
32 Daniel St., Portsmouth NH 03801
www.ppressbooks.com

Library of Congress Control Number: 9781958669037

Printed in the United States of America

For Jason, Celeste, Nina, Johnny, Eliot, Torrey, Alice, and Summer
because they bring me joy

Acknowledgements

All gratitude to the literary journals publishing my poems. The author gratefully acknowledges the Best of the Net's nomination for "Thinking about the Violence." Chard deNiord, Tom Sleigh, and Rodney Jones are some but not all of the gifted and patient poets who have guided my work. Deep thanks to my interns, my readers, and my mentor, Tom Lux.

Poet's Notes

Invention of 'Thrums' as a poetic form has driven Bedell's work
in the last several years. Thrums are those threads left on the loom
once a tapestry is removed. They are the poem's last line: the zap,
crux, or its essence. Although Bedell often writes in the thrum format,
she occasionally uses traditional when the poem requires.

Contents

What You Make of It

it came from everywhere
marshmallow fluff
white froth lulling but strong
up the cement stairs

today the tide is high

Nature's Dichotomy

longed for heat from the death of winter
earth turning rich brown from previous
ashen cheeks of shivered bodies
now red with pulsing vessels

moist earth replete with possibilities
sounds of sky grappling with weather
darkening but not foreboding

pending storm succulent air
ozone sweet and powerful
fragrance fills the backyard

every leaf moves slightly
in a dance of lightness
surrounded by soft fullness

tops of the white pine proudly flaunt
light green cylinders of newness
point away from dark inner branches

newness and old strength waving in tandem

Perseverance

dogwood white jumps out
brighter than before
blossoms held above the leaves
like a bride's bouquet

will she go down the aisle?
or perhaps say "no"
not to venture into the new

the old maple tree
covered with lichen
is not worried
even with a branch torn
the encrusted tree will survive

every sweet smelling molecule brings
portent auguring change
but nature's moves are unpredictable
vast frequent conflict of hot and cold
bring more new and violent storms

where is asylum?

Grampy's Legacy

I

Grampy's easy chair frayed threads
he long gone gold framed
photographs left in the living room

everyone was thrilled when he visited
he and nana drove up from Worcester
had a new Chrysler with electric windows

when she started having trouble spelling
in the middle school mother said
that's no problem Grampy is dyslexic

after that she made it into
8R2 the second highest
ranked class in the grade

she depressed wanted to get out of her tiny
New Hampshire town they decided
she would have to change her school

the parents found one for her
but it was tons of money
hard to afford it

II

but she did fine
bought a house
Grampy's legacy

she came back from the funeral
looked at his chair

sitting there with comfy arms
beautiful blue woven fabric

raised square motif
of thick beige threads

all worn down
to desecrated stubs

his love still unconditional
still unchanging

High Tide at Chapman's Landing

an empty old Chevy hitched to a
home-made trailer loaded with two saw horses
held together by new Phillips head screws

a young tattooed couple dressed in black
pulled up their sedan he removed two kayaks
while she screwed the paddles together

down by the ramp a handsome man thick dark hair
is in the sea grass up to his boots next to him
a bucket with three white perch swimming

wide grasses of the Piscataqua River sweep
while harried souls sleep

Egyptian Goose

under the acacia tree
two parents and two kids

they walk out onto the street
stand in the middle

a lady in her car stops
shoos all of them

the male looks at her
doesn't move

they all have a dark brown ring
around the bill the eyes and

a large stately brown polka dot
on the majestic beige chest

they moved one step
another car came by

honked like crazy
less patient than the first

risk to life not recognized
stupid but spectacular

Cormorant

Black tail feathers and top of the body, their wings are two-toned
half grey half black. They eat a variety of fish, salamanders,
shrimp, sometimes snakes, and even plant material. From the
estuary's surface, they launch all the way down to the bottom.

Unlike most seabirds cormorant's feathers lack the usual oils.
They land and spread their wings high and wide to dry,
to maintain their buoyancy.

They can not fly when their wings are wet.

North Rain, South Rain

driven by Bahama winds
such power knocks over
patio chairs

wetter than other rain
must run for shelter
makes you huddle together

New Hampshire rain
cold harsh Nor'easter
comes down from Canada

70 miles per hour
heavy wet snow
blinding blizzards

hunker down
safe in the house
removed from nature

the same horror
just different latitudes

Worms Can Save Us

Dean started the restaurant because he wanted to please his beloved Grandmother, who loved the Earth. Drove over to Tampa, found the Tampa bait shop and bought a bag of worms. A week later drove back and bought a bucket of them.

The worms were fed a mixture of macerated food waste, along with shredded paper cardboard and liquid. They like to eat food that is roughly half carbon and half nitrogen. Rich food is nearly all nitrogen. Poor quality paper is all carbon. The theory is the mix of nutrients increases the worm's reproductive rate.

They eat through the compost and their waste is an optimal soil enricher. Worms especially like cantaloupe, watermelon, and pumpkin, not human manure, meat scraps, fat, or tobacco.

Dean said, "I'm building an army for the sake of the Earth."

Fiesta Banner

a Maine teenager's brother
came back from hiking K-2

excited by the prayer flags he said,
"In Nepal they hang them all over the place,

the wind blows their prayers and mantras
bringing good will and compassion,

throughout the mountains
magnifying soulful power.

Basic goodness won't be seen or owned
by anyone yet is present for all forever."

the teen went to the cheap party shop
because her uncle had survived cancer

the entire family had flown in from all
over the US to celebrate his survival

she wanted something very special
saw a bunch of blue, white, red, green, yellow

flags strewn on a table the salesman said,
"Aren't those cool? They're the Nepalese

prayer flags. They believe the zen design
gives reverent blessing and healing."

after the party she went out on the deck
her heart was filled as she looked at

the lightly floating flags
center design starting to wither

but in Nepal they don't rip

After the Flood

The call came from her neighbor Denise at 6:30 in the morning.
"Do you know there are seven fire trucks in front of your house?"

"No I don't." In her nightgown she grabbed a bathrobe ran down
the stairs to the street. The chief fireman strode up to her.

"We have it under control Miss. There's a burst water pipe upstairs.
Get your valuables out of the house. Do you have anywhere to go?"

She did as she was told, grabbed clothes, her pocketbook and car keys.
Water flooded out of a window.

Finally after too much negotiation, the insurance company agreed to
put her up. One night she left the hotel to check on her home. But the
diner next door had a good ole blaring rock n' roll party going on. When
she got into her car instead of driving straight back to her construction
site she pulled into the diner. The music was hot. She got out and danced
with the crowd.

Before the next set she went up to the lead guitar, "I love your tunes."

The singer, bearded with a ripped t-shirt, grinned. "Thanks Doll."

"Would you ever play at my house?"

"Sure babe. Just tell me when."

A month later the band showed up. Set up in the backyard. Started with "There's a Bad Moon on the Rise."

Deep into the night a young buff cop stormed down the driveway. "There have been noise complaints from several people on the street." Her band kept playing the Clarence Clearwater Revival.

It was a shock but the people continued dancing, children still walking through the crowd and dogs looking for treats.

In the midst of the furor a 16-year-old wearing a flaming red bandeau strutted down the driveway, halted the officer and said, "Really."

All Works Out in the End

as we age our bodies decline
acute foot pain generates
breathless pain

found a Jungian
psychologist betrayed
patient by causing tinnitus

had a beautiful spot
in sunny Florida chose
superintendent

of schools to drive her
car down crashed it
in North Carolina

car was towed off 95
his friend drove up to unload
her belongings from the car

the state of Florida
wrote her a letter
notice of uninsured vehicle

she called her insurance agent
said "Please send proof of my
insurance to the state"

"It's no problem" said the agent
"And you know you have a
rental car provided"

the policy she chose covered her needs

Holly and the Alligator

fervently glad, finally they got property on the water
with glass wall sliders all across the living room

showing the canal   one day as they were looking out
on the mound of grass coming up from their water

a large scaly alligator
sprawled out of the estuary

laid the on the grassy mound
right next to the slider

"Jesus Christ," George screamed, "there's an alligator on our property."
Holly comes running, answering, "We have to call the State."

"Don't be stupid," George huffed, "it'll go away." "The monster
could smash into our living room," Holly screeched.

Holly couldn't find the number for the State.
George picked up her phone and finally got it.

an automated computer answered their call
they held for 20 minutes

the State lets them down
no response at all

six hours of stress   watching the gator sleep
they finally resorted to bed

the next morning   the monster was gone

Help

While watching James Corden Late Late Show, he saw a rectangular blue light down the river. Decided to go outside to search for what it was. Next door there was a construction site in the marina parking lot. Straining to find what the light was about, he tripped over a curb.

Got home pressed clean water on his wounds, took a sleeping pill went to bed. In the morning he woke to blood all over his fancy Cuddledown sheets. Called his GP at 8:30 no answer tried again two times. When he looked in the mirror he saw his face was badly abraded and his lip was swollen, perpendicular to the floor.

Called his dermatologist who could see him at 9 am. The waiting room was full but the doctor got him in by 9:30. He prescribed two antibiotics, one an ointment and the other pills. "You need x-rays for your cranial bones, both hands and knees. You need to get a script from your GP."

Since the GP was not answering the phone he went into the office all bloodied. Standing there the receptionist said, "Do you have an appointment?" He answered, "No I don't but I need one. Look at me." "I have nothing for you." An hour later a Medical Practitioner saw him and wrote a script for the x-rays.

He had to go home because there was no time in the x-ray office until 4:15. He managed to get home and drive back later. When finished the receptionist said, "We will have them for you in 48 hours."

Three days later they did not have the results. He felt alone, angry, frustrated and full of pain. Where is the Hippocratic Oath?

Trip Down South

in days of old stories of violence
tales of Georgia cops
folks beaten up because of race

her grandfather told stories about
going to the beaches
got pulled over

by a buff Georgia cop wearing blue shades
who asked "any liquor in the car?"
then beat the crap out of him

she got hungry on the drive down
stopped by a cool dock with a food shack
saw a nearly naked tan man

martini glass back meets
the edge of his neck
diagonals spread wide

evolved into oblong
biceps like the view of a
Nepalese mountain upside down

then he turned, thick muscle
connected to his rounded shoulder
perfect breasts raised high

below his collarbone two dark
aureoles with a delectable
pointed nipple waiting for a lick

his shades just the same as the Georgia cop

Unrequited Love

It took a month. They met once a week. An hour drive, she had searing pain. She was worried, terrified she'd need surgery.

He said, "We need an x-ray." She answered, "That's the least of my trouble, like living in the big city."

"I went to the University of Toronto. People don't realize how good a school it is," he replied. "I have dual citizenship. Then I went to the University of Pennsylvania."

"Guess what so did I," she giggled. "I hated being in the city. It was too loud. Distracting, just like when my son couldn't get multiplication. But he eventually got into a really good Quaker School." He looked into her green eyes, fiery just like her curly hair. "But now he's fine, in a Fortune 500."

Long pause, arms spread out wide he answered, "My son is a big deal too." They both grinned.

He said, "We could talk forever."

Betrayed just like in death she said, "You are taken I am not."

A Thing

she made it all the way home
still the back pain, hip and elbow

he had called her every other day
the first time was last Tuesday

he couldn't hear her she was at the apple store "I'd like to take
you to dinner I'm free today, Wednesday or Thursday

she had a computer group so Wednesday was a "no" when she
pulled into the restaurant he was standing there tall and cute

she wore tight capris, a cami under her see-through flocked shirt
got a better feeling about this first date than others

next he wanted to go out on "Saturdee" night
she was surprised he was asking so soon

A trip to the moon on gossamer wings
Just one of those things

Relentless

cold, foggy and dark
stone jetty makes a curve for the tide

it is only their third date
and a Saturday night

she was much younger
he was too old for all of this

but she had said "dinner was a super hoot"
then invited him to see her new app

he was intrigued with the technology
spent 50 years as an engineer

they drove to the inlet
wind lashed the water

she ran out reached the jetty's cement end
he watched her go

*I just bought this hibiscus shirt too much money
to get it drenched* he thought

he went back to his car
she could not see him

the Orion Nebula showed clear on her phone
but in the black darkness

he was entirely gone
she couldn't find him

tip-toed back through the puddles
when she reached him, no kiss

she wondered *is he impotent?*

After the Swim

he hated this
his dude days were gone

like an out-of-date
straw cowboy hat

no longer a stud
wet and powerless

Island Rhythm

long with a narrow width rectangular pool
so one could look across and gauge outfits

many wrought iron tables with lion's paw legs
girls wearing hats and large necklaces

seated on those tricky chairs from Paris
woven in white

basket-weave design brick floor surrounds the pool
bougainvillea blooming magenta

half way up a five story building
real flowers everywhere

except the pergola the length of one side of the pool
dripping down variegated vines and orchids

all fake where no one would notice
couples filling couches under the palm trees

drinking snowbird cocktails
smelling of fresh chopped pineapple

dude with close cropped hair
silk shirt with black diamond-edged jacket

matching socks peeking out from his capri pants
velvet flats with embroidered Gucci horse bits

girlfriend with flowing leopard skirt
silver spaghetti strap top

two guitars tall island drums and a rare wooden
flat rectangular instrument played like a bongo

a four-year-old boy with preppy parents
wearing a monogrammed shirt walks

across holding his penis

Local Vision

in Hawaiian
jams
cracker ponytail

staggers out
from the waves
yanks out his hair tie

wet hanging tendrils
down to his
chest hairs

speckled like a Florida cuckold

Pink Polo

Back in the day a bunch of female executives got together once a month. It was hard in the summer because it was so humid but everyone had a great garden. The head of the Philadelphia HUD gave the party in August.

"I have a special game for us. I'm sure you all know about Penn's special club, the Mask and Wig. The magazine editor Jane added, "Oh yeah where all the men dress up like women. Do you think they're all gay?" She laughed naughtily.

"We're all going to sit around and eat fish off my oven platters, given to me at the wedding." They all laughed hysterically at the concept of wedding gifts.

"As I pass the flag, you are going to tell us what a man would wear to make you want to fuck him immediately." Jane shouted, "Pink Lacoste polo shirt, khaki shorts that you can see up to the jewels. Of course tassel loafers with no socks. We like naked feet." she giggled.

Fast forward 40 years Jane went to negotiate a difficult car insurance deal. Her car was hit by a giant Porsche SUV and she needed someone smart. His directions to the office were simple. "I am right by the car wash."

She was 20 minutes late. He didn't realize there was another car wash in the next mini mall. "Sorry I am late there was another car wash." He looked up from behind his desk and was wearing a pink polo and beige Bermudas.

She Was Not That

Roman met her a month before his wife died. She walked into his shop wearing short shorts and a tee shirt. Eyes and arms flashing around like lightning bugs in summer. Julie asked, "Whenever you finish the couch will be great. I'm away the last week in August for vacation on an island where everyone skinny-dips." He noticed it wasn't a question. She confused him. "Where is that?" "Lake Winnipesaukee," Julie grinned. He finished her couch early. When Roman was to deliver it he phoned, left a message, "There's been a change, I have to deliver your couch late…on Thursday. Uh. A tragedy happened. I'm sure you'll understand."

He stunned her a week later. "My wife was hit by a truck getting onto 125." Julie felt pity. "Oh, how horrid. Should I take you to lunch?" "I'll have to call you back," he said. "Of course," she hung up. His lanky body and those sprightly eyes roused more than steam and confusion.

Though that was a year ago, he had never left her. In her mind. The couch had wrinkles and a hump where the back met the arm. When she got back to town she phoned. Spoke to his machine. In five minutes he called. "Got your message. Right back at you." At that moment Julie felt a bolt jet through her chest. The lightning was still there.

When they were dancing close in the kitchen she asked, "What are you after?"
He countered, "What are you after?" Julie looked up at him surprised, reacted,
"Maybe some dating." Roman managed, "No." She poured him another glass
of wine, ushered him into the front room, pointing at the bumpy couch he'd
made for her. They, for a minute, sat silent. The babe responded using her best,
level voice, "I'm not a one night stand." He inspected her carefully then spoke,
"I only go out one night a week and that is with the country music group."
He stung her. "Then what is tonight?" Her tsunami rose like the volcano
disintegrating much of Southeast Asia. "I don't know," he answered.
They made small talk for a bit. She stood up. He left.

She was not his slut.

He Fell in Love Over the Internet

she had thick dark curly hair standing in front
of the jungle with a body as hot as the air

he had bleached blonde hair
undercut with the touch of a buzz making sexy long top hair

he loved that she was a naughty writer explicit novels
she loved that he cared about the environment

he admitted he worked on the Alaska pipeline
she confessed that she won an award

in his picture he was standing by a metal rig with his dog
one of her photos showed her in a skimpy tennis dress with a victory smile

quite quickly he gave her his phone number but admitted he had trouble
with reception because he was in the Bering Strait, Alaska

"I'm coming home next week. Can't think about anything but
you making dinner in my kitchen."

Oh baby, you've got the wrong woman. I don't cook.

Silver Internet I

they met on site
she was pleased he didn't send that stupid little smile
tired of men too lazy to type a sentence

at last finally he invited her out
he asked her to come to Manchester which
she didn't know at all

parked her car in the handicap spot put her bag
of cushions for the bad back on the floor
no sign of the kindly looking gray-haired guy

she got a text "Are you here? I'm by the door."
he showed her to a table inside "I used to come
here for lunch when I was working."

she was surprised the conversation flowed well
"I guess I should ask if you're married."
his honest blue eyes looked up "My wife left.

She came in to go to bed said
'I can't do it anymore' and walked out."
he paused "There'll never be another as good as her."

Well he can't date me. That's the end of him.

Silver Internet II

he was from out-of-state
"it's no problem" he said "I go up
there by you a lot because I like
to antique shop."
next phone call after some chat
he says "how about lunch?"
she said "what day are you thinking?"
he says "I'm busy all week."
she says "me too" *such a fuck*
"how about Saturday?"

and now he wants to come up
he asks "where should we go?"
"there's a classic New Hampshire place"
she answered "called the Wentworth."

"how about 12:30?"
"sounds great"
they hung up
she thought this guy could be a super fuck
her friend said make sure you go to a public
place and drive your own car
that was no problem

sent her a text saying "it's not right. not coming on Saturday. sorry."

Carol's Dilemma

the most popular girl in town
got pregnant by Bert

the mothers gossiped
"Mary Ann out to here."

went to the prom anyway with him
got a special dress

at the corner Rexall's everyone
was trying the new cherry coke

the bad boys said "Ah we get to taste
more cherries than Bert."

another girl's mom had just delivered a baby
exhausted from forty-eight hours of labor

asked her oldest to buy nipples and bottles
"What?" "Go to Rexall's and get me the stuff for the baby."

her daughter moaned and hopped onto her bike
all the cool kids were at Rexall's

parked motorcycles all over the storefront
she asked the soda jerk "I need a bottle."

he said "You mean a cherry coke?"
"No I need bottles, baby bottles."

all the hoods turned and gasped
the next day the word was out

Carol was buying baby bottles, she'd had
a baby just like Mary Ann

Big Sex

Two hours late for the drive down there. My radio blared love songs from the Phantom of Opera, another Broadway hit I missed in 1985. That greener grass in someone else's yard. He'd been worried so it seemed a good idea to give it one more try. Small sweet tonguings when we walked to the bedroom, repeated and repeated like Jazz licks. I curled under as my female fuzzed with warmth. He went for my bra like an adolescent eager but fumbling. A vehement pinch at the hooks, then shook it off. Some smooth touch across the top of my breasts. Some nipple squeezes. We went next to the bed, discussed condoms (I'd forgotten them). "Wait I've got a sample," he said. At last we lay down. Armageddon approach. The room was some tropical color. The ceiling pearl. A 50s hula hoop propped behind the wide brass bed. Its bright striped plastic jarred against the fruitiness of the peach paint. He was huge – too big for the condom. With complete dogged determination I pushed and tugged to roll it on. Yes. He got me ready with his fingers, then his mouth. Finally he went in me very slowly, softly, soft like The Cryptique Aire Twelfth Night Suite. Just the tip at first. He didn't want to hurt me like the last time. Felt as good as the Orion shinning in the dulcet darkness. It was two months since anyone's been there. Then he made it all the way in. Not clumsy like the tennis court, but here the long soar, covering me more than I knew. Enveloped in the Third Movement Erotica No 3 Crescendo.

Not the Man

Paraplegic shrink said
"I never liked him, he
pitched my hospital.
Odd, too cause
I like most people."

That was the guy who left me

Weezie

Small northern island in a Great Lake, the Outdoors Club had changed occupancy to 45 due to Covid. Same mahogany launch, same ride to the Island's dock. Even the people the same: all nature-lovers, all environmentally sensitive, with only a few exceptions.

The Sunday Sing, no longer indoors but on the dock. Good ole folk songs. Very talented singers, three part harmony in the mountain air, sweet and powerful.

Afterwards he came up next to her put his hand on her hip, not aggressive, rather a wave of warmth. They walked off together lost in the crowd. The next day he started hollering "Weezie" past all 45 people at the dining tables.

Since many on the island had come for generations she felt natural making conversation with him. She, herself, had come for 60 years. After lunch she bravely asked, "Are you from here?" "Yup," he grinned. She continued, "I might know your family." He froze, leaned closer and said, "My Dad is dead." Startled she blurted, "I'm so sorry." He read her carefully, thought she was OK, added, "No he's not." Now stunned she answered, "You are a liar." The young staff were all there. Yup they said, "That's him!"

Later in the week at the "I Never Expected" Circle Event the stories amazed all 45 people. It lasted into nightfall. He placed his arm around her waist to guide her off the dock. Automatically she reached over but he was taller so it landed on his butt. Like a glorious rock, such a fine hard sphere. Instantly she moved it up, unsure of him.

The next day on the dock he sat near the water slide as if he were a lifeguard. She checked him out, fit confident, maybe a smart ass. "Can you make me a lifeguard sign?" His tone was blunt.

"You mean lifeguard on duty?" she asked. "Yup but the printing has to be perfect." His tone was serious. *How presumptuous. I am doing him a favor* she thought. Then she heard her voice say, "Okay."

She was an artist so it was no big deal. It was easy to figure out the sizes of the letters and the spacing. It was gorgeous. She walked over to him, half naked with a perfectly tight body. When she presented it he said, "Nice."

At the Water Carnival the whole island gathered, hoping they'd again have the canoe race around the float like in the past. A couple was in a canoe together with the wife in the stern blindfolded. The husband had to give her directions on where to go. Always someone crashed into another boat or even into the float. The crowd loved it.

She saw the flirt dive into the water and swim across past the float over to the other island. When he returned and climbed out of the water, his divine blonde hair was flattened. What a turn-off. But then he rubbed it with his towel and pushed it straight back. So it stood straight up. A flashback to the old BrylCreem ads from the sixties. She was now ready. But he was not. He walked away to the Launch House. Still that night he shouted "Weezie" down the long dining tables. *Was he a dick?*

The next morning by the Launch House all the wait staff were hanging out. He, across the deck, shouted at her, "Glad I met you but you're 40 years too old." Not a woman to take any crap she hit back with, "And you're just the right age for me!" Everyone laughed. *Why would someone say that in the midst of a crowd? Was he a prick?*

She was chatting with her friend the baker. The kid came up and stood there, hovering. He wanted her attention. "Where do you live?" he talked over the baker. She reached up to calm him. Because of all the time on the dock she was familiar with his chest. His abs were flat unlike most fit men. Her subconscious kicked in. She stroked his shoulder, then explored his neck, still talking to her friend. He had stubble from his grown-out haircut. She unconsciously stroked the bristle. That was hot even though she had conducted many earlier studies of his body. This previously unnoticed phenomenon was now fun and intriguing.

When she finished her chat, he asked, "I heard you write books. What kind?" Now she carefully checked his meaning out. "Yup rowdy fiction." "That's good," he responded, grinning. "Do you have any here?" "Yup."

Then in her cabin he puzzled looking over the cover. "It's Mars, the rivulets," she explained. "Wow," he swooped down.

Great kisses and more. It'd been a long time for her. And it was long. Later they agreed, "We'll talk on the phone." She was leaving the Island. Grinning she said, "I'm free Tuesday at 7." He answered, "OK."

On the last day most people streamed down to the launch. Goodbyes were cherished. Wonderful waving and shouts to dear friends as the boat left. He wasn't there.

At home Tuesday came, he didn't call.

Family Event

The family was close. Everyone felt jubilant. Their mother was beside herself to have them all in the building. The young boys had had Christmas parties in their school classrooms. Judy the oldest had just driven up from New York. Natalie hadn't seen her daughter in four months.

"Thanks so much Mom for the poster," said Daniel. "I love Impressionism." Natalie had bought him a Monet Water Lilies poster for his room at college. She had hoped that the water would bring him joy.

"Oh Mom, that poster swirls around me every day. The green strokes in the water come down and give me chills. The black under the lily pads creeps me out."

Judy, his sister, was horrified. His behavior reminded her of homeless people ranting on the corner by her apartment.

She followed her Mom into the kitchen and said, "Mom, I am worried about Daniel. That business about the poster was pretty strange."

Natalie was shocked, but wanted to hide her fear. Usually chatty, she was silent for a minute and a half. "I have the perfect idea. We'll all go on a ski trip and he knows how to ski." She grinned and grabbed Judy's shoulder. But Judy pulled back just a little. Felt uneasy from her toes to the top of her head.

Years later he was discharged from the hospital, his meds were working well. The family came together again. Same house same living room, but this time Daniel was back.

"The Road Not Taken"
for Robert Frost

He went into the woods for forty days and forty nights, just like he remembered from Sunday School. There was a dirt road through a dark gray canyon lined with impenetrable granite rocks. There were small pebbles under his feet, just like his list of overwhelming trouble.

After the demanding climb up the hill, his legs ached. He lay down in a patch of partridge berries. The smooth small leaves and the red fruit cheered his weary spirit. He turned around.

Walked slowly kicking the pebbles out of his way. The path flattened, he noticed a narrow stream, went to it. Put his hand in.

The water was icy but spotted with hope. He decided to go home.

The Indictments of Evil

Selma   violation of the right of freedom to vote

Jack the Ripper   violation of the right for liberty of life

Jeffrey Epstein   violation against humanity

Olaf the Art Consultant

The Palm Beach Art Show was always at the Convention Center.
The entrance was stunning lined on both sides with human-sized topiary.
The audience filled the hall with all ages of women studded with large
diamond jewelry, men both gay and straight dressed in Designer, some straight
ones wore pink jackets or pants most gay ones wore highest line radical design.

She stood there looking at this weird boat painting. The top third was harsh
orange. The boat was abstract, long and powerful maybe some kind of
freighter. On the bottom third there was nothing but white canvas, a line
and a squashed oval circle.

"What do you think of this?" a male voice interrupted her thoughts.
Startled she turned, "I don't know yet." He remarked, "I like the boat."
He bent over to look more closely. "No, it's not just a boat it's a symbol of
the military industrial complex." He looks at her blankly. She observes his
shirt, nice fabric tricky simple collar. She loved the white and red wine stripes.
"I think it's a triptych," she added. "The boat has no detail it's definitely a
symbol and the white canvas unpainted below, it has nothing." He answered,
"No there is a line and that circle. Could be artist signature." She noticed
his foreign accent.

"You see the solid orange above the boat?" She continued, "I think this part
is like New York Abstract Art." She perplexed him. "Perhaps you know
about the abstract expressionists who used solid colors?"

"Come to the café with me. Wine is good." When they sat down, she peeked at his groin. Pleased to see it was covered with burgundy velvet. "My Dad was artist." She listened intensely. "I am artist. I am art restorer."

"How cool," she gushed. "Paint is bad," he stated. "Lead poisoning is why Van Gogh died," she responded. He stared at her incredulous. "What do you paint?" "Before mainly Greek Orthodox now work in gallery." She noticed his broken English.

"I'm from Kyiv." "Oh, yikes that's in the news." "Yes there is much. My sister just took my mother out of Ukraine." "I am really glad to hear that." She looked into his eyes.

"I've done yoga most days." He stares right at her. "What about you?" "Oh, thirty years or so. I love it." Surprised he said, "I see white when I do it."

He had set his cell phone on the table. It did not look like hers. It rang. He spoke quickly into it. "I've got to go. May I give you my card?" She looks it over. It had pictures of small odd beads one with a Chinese portrait on it. "When would you like me to call?" "You call me anytime."
He looked deep into her, turned and left.

She decides against it.

Never Again
Letter to Vladimir Putin March 7, 2022

Invasion of a sovereign country in the 21ˢᵗ century feels familiar to those of us who immigrated to the US, escaping German Nazism. Armaments raised against innocent men, women, and children remind us of sirens in the night, fire bombing the streets and destruction of cities.

Millions died to defeat fascism in World War II, in an effort to provide the world protection from autocratic absolute rulers. The battle was won for preservation of the individual, freedom of movement, national safety and justice.

And we will prevail.

Strength in the Time of Covid

On the celestial equator, Orion's constellation is visible throughout
the world. One of the most recognizable and pronounced constellations
in the night sky. Orion is the handsome hunter valued in Greek mythology.
His stance is strong. Steady and firm, one leg bent the other straight, as
he shoots his arrows. His foot lit by the star Nigel. Nigel is a blue supergiant
that will become an explosive supernova. Orion's stance gives him infinite power.
Orion stands steady over humanity. Giving constant assurance.

We look up and find his strength.

Also by Bedell Phillips

POETRY

Edges of Waves
Thrums & Tapestry
Wolf Tail Glimmer
Is There Life

PROSE

Around the Bend

www.ingramcontent.com/pod-product-compliance
Lightning Source LLC
Chambersburg PA
CBHW022343040426
42449CB00006B/698